Jane Weir

The Way
I Dressed
During
The Revolution

Templar Poetry

First Published 2005 by Templar Poetry

Nevertheless, 2 Catcliffe Cottages,
Bakewell, Derbyshire DE45 1FL

ISBN 0-9550023-2-X

A CIP catalogue record for this book is available
from the British Library.

Typeset by Pliny
Graphics by Weir-Woolf
Printed and bound in India

823.92

For Dr Pauline Polkey

Like a polka dot pattern I persist

CONTENTS

ACKNOWLEDGEMENTS

Acknowledgments are due to the editors of the following publications in which some of these poems first appeared: *Out of Fashion (Faber & Faber), PN Review, In Verse, Poetry Nottingham, Writing on Water (Ragged Raven Press), Petra Kenny International Poetry Competition Anthology.*
Thanks to Simon Armitage and Carola Luther (*Walking the Animals, Carcanet 2004*) for their support.

The author wishes to thank the Platt Hall Costume Museum, Manchester for access to their collection of stomachers. Thanks are also due to Alex McMillen for advice, criticism and support.

The author wishes to acknowledge support from Arts Council England, which has facilitated the completion of this work.

THE MESSAGE

Innocents, we circumnavigate five counties,
come sleepwalking to this slumbering place
guided by a blazing star, bearing inadequate gifts.
We breathe its air,
smitten with your motes of savage poetry.
It must have been the car wheels trundling
over the cattle grid that triggered, roared out
to you we'd crossed the border.

Tremors radiated from our feet, as we stepped
over the donkey stone step. The house is a puzzle,
each room has its own pieces, all rooms are difficult
to settle in. We dig, earth ourselves in as you set to,
thickening your territory. At about midnight we curl
like ammonites in bed, you unleash one of your elements.
Wind gurns, bellows, rattles the slates like a giant poppy
seed head. We pay attention. The pitiful moon lounges,

a florin on the lid of the night sky, electroplates the skylight.
Through the blinding ink wash we watch as sheep appear,
float luminous as Chinese lanterns over our heads,
then disappear, like a weird rhyme. Much later
the wind drops, blots the trees and hills. We edge closer.
You sent odd gusts to plague us. We see their silhouettes,
necklaces made from small mammals, carrions torn
from the throats of hedges, hear them splatter

against the glass, a warning to any pretenders.
We say we understand, we do. We get the message, we do.
Though second time round, I feel myself detach, hesitate.

HAT

The valency of your face framed by the open door.
Her hat I will talk about before it's off your lips,
parted lips that wear a day-night deal, hankering
after her hat, and her head that holds her hat,
masses of hair that block the moulded felt
blue, ease the band of burgundy a little.

Our hands in collaboration. Come in off the street.
I pretend you have nothing to tell me. Sit down.
Your tongue is bud-less, so much so, the fine
saliva stitching has worn away a soft pink.
I've seen her too. Her face has the priority

of silks, her body the plain severity of space,
Derry boots hold the shine of her ankles footfall.
Stand up, let's talk, let's walk around the table.
You're younger, she's older.
I gave you *Sentimental Education*, you chucked it back.
Open fire, tender buttons of rain. We're here again.

Set up the glasses. I'll get the Jamesons out.
Cut tendons. You slip. Tell me what I already know.
You've been round. You loll, a top button open.
She's cinema against the sash. Slight resist. So she gives
like pastel on stone. Autumn kiss. I am silent about
my mouth on her mouth on your mouth, silkscreen print.

RECOVERING

When I cough no matter whether
it's short and raspy or endless
like a marching army on slush and ice,
you're attentive. You always get up,
answer with a look, always follow
up with deft touches.
Half awake I watch you light
our bedroom fire- the room's
Moscow in winter.
You pull up a stick chair, open
your serious book. I silhouette
the side of your face with my eyes
and think of Tolstoy,
your other family, our child
who's due in a month.

Now that I'm slowly getting better
you surprise me, etch my name
in ice on the window pane,
investing in a still from my favourite film.
Today you bring a wad
of sunflowers into the room.
I am full of sleep,
secretly you had positioned them
so that when I wake
I can observe them
from our bed, their petals tigering
through an alchemy of winter light.

4

If spies had pressed their faces
to the glass they would have seen us.
We were the two figures skating.

HAEMORRHAGE

She pushes away his hand
that offers her ice to swallow,
as though a bell had struck,
or shutters had clacked,
acted slapstick against
the sides of crumbling plaster,
or a child's voice
had lifted, as it turned
a corner, cast itself
into the burnt sienna air,
like pigeons in an Italian square.
Primeval. She kept saying to herself,
I did it, I did it, a glorious litany.
Then she took it upon herself
to be her own sweet torturer,
and pinched herself,
God knows how many times,
sank down on her knees,
heavenly, like a virgin again,
sole witness to visions at a well,
a serial of purple bruises to tell,
before she was sure, as sure
as she could be, that she'd been harsh
as an ice age, flint- napping
her way, throwing off
the rotting carcass of him,
her searing arctic breath
enough perma for him
to pack his bags, leave.

BUSBY BABES

People talk about the day Kennedy was shot,
ask where you were, what you were doing
at the time, but it means nothing to me.
See I was working, I'd just finished the last batch,
when a man flew in, carrion crow in blue overalls,
scything his arms, his voice tide-bearing.

And surely it was some crazy sick joke
that wasn't funny anymore, wouldn't somebody
put it out of its misery, words fitting on the factory floor.
Accounts got their tranny out, huddled round,
but the sky muscled in like a bouncer,
arm locking all transmissions from Winter Hill.

So me and Marina we pelted it down the stairs,
and in the panic one of us lost our shoe in our rush
to out the truth. Joining the mob, we spilt onto the street,
rapidly filling with print, raining sensational sleet.
We breached the barricade, where a lad looking
like he'd just done ten years and stepped out

onto civvy street was reading out loud
to a massing crowd, from an early edition,
as though we were illiterate and couldn't read.
Its what we seemed to need, and words like
promising, a lost generation, all local lads,
lived within a stones throw of the city-walls,

kept regurgitating, until we were gagging on it.
Some bloke in the crowd kept shouting out,
scanning swarms in the air for death lists.
And I kept thinking please, please don't let it be Byrne,
and I could see her thinking the same only a different name,
Edwards. Then the streetlights struck at us

hard in the face, blinding like an own goal,
and the massing crowd rushed forward.
Mythic river, it swept us off our feet,
and we linked arms to stabilise ourselves.
And the lament that came out of our mouths
was like a Greek city state, knee deep in mourning.

MY MOTHER SAYS CAN SHE COME FOR A FEW DAYS

I hear her voice inside my head,
unseasonal, torrential, swollen
as a river after his voice,
a months rainfall fallen in two hours.
She'll be here midday.
I make up a bed,
and as in war time, re-jig the raw
ingredients for tonight's dinner.
I tell myself not to say anything,
when she walks through the door,
a different generation, this is not
what she wants or expects.
I think to myself, it's a lot to swallow,
his words, actions, like foreign bodies
they'll pass through her, given time.
Later, brushing by her bedroom door
I stifle the impulse to rush in,
give her the homecoming that as a girl
of twelve she saw, so often
described to me, her Father strolling
up the street, home from active service
in the civil war in Greece,
with Monty in North Africa.
Sepia life, the lot dumped
with his kit bag by his side,
the pair of them a garland after the war.

HAND KNITS

Remember the chunky gloves, scarves,
the mis-shaped jumpers,
the one year someone had a stab
at a bright orange balaclava.
A job lot, or so we thought, all jumbled up
scarred, marred like broken biscuits on the market.
Discarded, we scattered them on the carpet
for the desperate ones, fledglings amongst us,
for fun to try on; and if we dared,
go round to our mates in.
We can't believe we thought like that.
These days with the onslaught of winter,
we roam the city, machine streets,
out-of- town factory shops feeling cheated,
though not defeated because we knit our own
or scour charity shops for the likes of the above,
that once we would have buried in a shallow grave,
or drowned in the gruel of a gravel pit.
We're pilgrims on a holy trail-
after that something that lifts, that sets us
apart like inches of stars from yards of dark,
for we've honed the gift that fisher folk
have of frisking, running their eyes across
a neck, over a shoulder, down the sleeve
to finger the cuff.

SARDINIAN POWDER COMPACT
I

We sit on the edge of the bed,
your fifties Antler suitcase
squats between us,
stubborn as a protester
intent on staging a sit in.

Travel labels hang on, held fast
by strips of sellotape sticking down
each country travelled through.
When you open the lid

the brittle edged labels
splinter like toffee made
with too much sugar.
You flick the shards away
with your fingernails.

I watch them drift, a lacy mix
like insect wings
infesting the air. Your fingers poised
on the outer perimeter of its base,

your other hand delves, aided
by your search light eyes, salvaging,
turning over the geometric innards
of the case lining like a bailiff.

Its close now, I know because
your bare shoulder blades twitch
like an impala. Here it is,
found in a cave, you hand it over.

I unzip the compact. A Bohemian oyster
shell, mirror cracked, eyeshot silver.
A ring of gauze, hymen where the powder
disc yellows, degrades, and opposite
a sponge anaemic as an unripe raspberry.

II

Why now? I thought you'd forbidden
that trivial hand held part of your past
from ever having direct contact with me.
I see you smiling, hiding his significance
behind your mirror, under your weak
laughter; that padded place where you
have kept him for so long.
Still I keep on asking, having
no way of knowing what happened
when you went out there -none at all-
so I improvise, starting with geography.

A year spent in Sardinia,
island of recovery, of lead, of salt,
a fuse wire of zinc veins
running through the mountains.
Where a mistral wind bellows,
bentwoods the trees and shrubs,
where you can walk along
a Sahara beach, a blue headband
of sea holding itself back from
a sprawl of dunes.

Was it here? Think. Can you place me?
Did you ride piggy back, adder
inland on the back of his Vespa,
stopping first to sip - religiously,

mint tea with his Mama,
feed each other as if through bars
sparacelli in padella?
And later, much later, did two of you
flee to the music of goats,
a Miro of dots and dashes,
then sink inside the dimpled
chin of an emptying hillside?

Was the sky thickening its colour
with its brood of clouds,
a varicose of lightning?
Were your rice paper clothes
dissolving, saturated
with the scents of cave, juniper, pine?
As outside you heard the staithe
creaks of holm oaks,
their branches arthritic,
swanning in the sweltering heat,
while inside the omen ticked.

CAT HAIRS ON YOUR TROUSERS

Three days before Armistice Sunday
and poppies had already been placed
on individual war graves. Before you left,
I pinned one onto your lapel, crimped petals,
spasms of paper red, disrupting a blockade
of yellow bias binding around your blazer.

Sellotape bandaged around my hand,
I rounded up as many white cat hairs
as I could, smoothed down your shirt's
upturned collar, steeled the softening
of my face. I wanted to graze my nose
across the tip of your nose, play at
being Eskimos like we did when
you were little. I resisted the impulse
to run my fingers through the gelled
blackthorns of your hair. All my words
flattened, rolled, turned into felt,

slowly melting. I was brave, as I walked
with you, to the front door, threw
it open, the world overflowing
like a treasure chest. A split second
and you were away, intoxicated.
After you'd gone I went into your bedroom,
released a song bird from its cage.
Later a single dove flew from the pear tree,
and this is where it has led me,

skirting the church yard walls, my stomach busy
making tucks, darts, pleats, hat-less, without
a winter coat or reinforcements of scarf, gloves.

On reaching the top of the hill I traced
the inscriptions on the war memorial,
leaned against it like a wishbone.
The dove pulled freely against the sky,
an ornamental stitch. I listened, hoping to hear
your playground voice catching on the wind.

THE FAMISHED

After she'd finally admitted
they were dead,
after the Planter relics
were handed out, money settled,
she committed herself
to sorting and bagging,
to writing whole lines, pages
with a proper ink pen and paper,
instead of churning out tableaux
of hieroglyphic thank you notes.

After she'd measured
the duration of the clock
for the last time,
risen from her chair, addressed
the uprising of her three
elder brothers - a racket
that eventually ceased-
she sank solemnly like a monster
beneath the brim of the loch
deep table and steadily
she began to speak.

A harness of sweet breath,
work horses nudging
at her palms for sugar cubes,
unrefined oats, they didn't
protest or make a mess,

but silently egged
her on, like a boxer's fist,
knowing she'd resist any impact,
detainment, persuasion of any sort.

Announcing, she'd take full
responsibility, she ordered
it be brought in, a platter
of bread and cheese
for all the burnt meals
they'd suffered as children.
All around the room the light
leaked, weakened by the sudden thaw
brought on by the sound,
the opening closing of jaws.

FULCRUM

A pale stencil of yourself,
you sit across from me,
your roots need doing,
your shoes, clothes set to neutral,
no longer suggest or dictate.
You do your best, make it hard
for me to tell what you're thinking.
It doesn't wash. I watch the way
your hands work inside the workshop
of your lap. You mime happy,
buffering the clasp of your fifties purse.

It hurts to see you like this.
Since you've retired he's upped
the errands, whittled a bigger
blackthorn stick, perfected his Olympic
throw, a fair distance for you to fetch.
I know. I want to tell you that I've
been awake, aware and many a time
felt the need, sword raised, to rush in,
rescue you. But your brothers,
later my husband, although up
in arms, they held me back.

I want to confess, how hard it's been
to draw back from the brink, brick
myself up, like a cat or a nun,
to mask this recurring testimony.

Looking at you now, I can't stand by
and watch like a sick supporter with
a season ticket. Tongue tied, suspended,
you reel and jig at what I'm saying.
Its up to you, I can cut you down,
smuggle you out, use the whole
of my body like a pendulum,
or on the count, bell ring from your legs.

A HANK OF YELLOW WOOL IN A LANDSCAPE

My boy and I skirt the churchyard walls,
graves gather us like smocking stitches.
Cable, chain, feather, Vandyke,
herringbone, stem honeycomb.
War graves click like white milk teeth.

We work amongst them, our feet step
left to right, taking up pleats of grass,
burls cling to our scarves.
We cannot walk in straight lines,
so we single hop here,
double step there, sometimes treble.
Light as muscovy feathers,
we swingboat across the puffy stones.

Reaching for the hill monument,
I sit on the bench, cut my boy loose
on the landscape. Wind blows cold
diamonds, braids; a hank of yellow
wool in a hollow startles me.
I call him over, we crouch, look.
Yellow buttercups our faces.

GRACE

Its not a bad place to sit and sew,
though the low beams depress me a bit,
especially when the light ducks and dives,
slinks like a civet across the floor boards:
then its tough work, threading a needle.
I take one break a day, usually when
she's secured and sleeping. If I'm late
they keep my dinner warm for me.
They know the score. It's not so bad,
I've my pipe and pint of porter waiting,
patient lovers by the hearthstone.
And it pays well, so I'm able to lay
something by. There's not many folks
round here can say that.
What? Someone's got to do it.
Listen, you'd be surprised how many
would seize at the chance should
a vacancy arise, slip comfortably
into my list slippers.
Under orders I do what I'm told.
You've got a nerve gawping at me.
I only do with manacles and chains
what others did to her with amorous
gifts of dresses and jewels.
Some days when she sits still,
listless as a mill pond and I drift
across her face, I wince as it pinches,
hints at our similarity. On nights

when the music rises from down
below I love to watch her
polar bear dance, pace and sway,
her skin and neck cracking, yellowing.
Some nights I play at being a courtier.
Freed up, she becomes my marmoset
to tease, feed with tit bits.
Some times we like to punish her visitors,
band of inquisitors. So I leave the candle
burning, door ajar. Curling my lip
I turn the other way as she quivers
on out into the passageway,
heaps of darkness succouring.

A PIECE OF DONEGAL CARPET

She is told of the fragment as she faces the sea.

From every part of the country come fields of woollens.
A dense garden party, heady with linseed,
and the purply heave of heather honey,
the stench of bees thick on Irish tweeds,
cut flowers, Donegal, Connemara.

She is asked if she wants it.

Fragments of land, flannel, serge, broadcloth, melton,
worked upon, hard as callus hands on a back.
Cheviot, saxony, pilot, vicuna, worsted cloth,
the tilled threads that mute colour, disrupt patterns,
not a thing to be looked upon or contemplated.

She is shown its quality by a gesture.

But she casts her cool eyes from wavering fingers,
and listens to them blooming.
The fancy curl suitings, trouserings, tweeds.
She imagines her seasoned floor, weighs the voices
the cleave, hack, and how the words might thrum.

She is assured several times of its uniqueness.

24

She could have it, hang it, perhaps place it
under light sensitive glass
or lay it between special sheets
to drift amongst her ancestors,
or lock it in her chest, but its too safe.

She reflects on its utility,

and rolls it out, breaking onto the floor
like a sad mouth losing its edge,
and she watching
it fray, unfurl
at the sight of her bleak brethren boots.

RECUPERATING 1913

What matters is that I'm here,
feel strong enough, so don't keep
her waiting, let her in.
Though I struggle to raise myself,
to rise from lying to sitting up in bed.
Kafuffle.I push them away.
My body is wracked, swimming
in saline, is white as veal, lies wrapped
and layered in sheets of filo.

A figurine you stand between
the columns of the door. I manage
a wave. Come on in, make room,
someone take those clothes from
off the chair. Settle yourself down,
get comfy; there. I signal with my
finger for you to hush, move your
head a little this way, keep still,
let my famished eyes feast at will.

Punctual as a moon you obey,
silver trace your face my way.
A moment is all it takes to capture
the memory of all of you in turn,
marching arm in arm in arm,
an anthem that spreads and spreads
before it passes on like a baton.
Like rhyming couplets let me savour
all of you and all the work you continue to do.

The afternoon disrobes, regiments
of cards daisy chain around
my bed in solidarity.
And as the light begins to fade
and lamps are lit, you start to read,
first the private papers, pamphlets,
then piles of lobby papers, first hand accounts,
prison diaries, petitions in brief, the heave
of that headline, the word on the street,
an editorial tone that picks up then drifts
like the sight of dragoons massing
at the edge of a crowd, blackening its mood.

And when you come to messages of solace
and support, once again I'm made aware
of what a difference to the spirit
an individual act, a pledge,
a gesture, like this rosette of tulips
arranged in a penny vase can make.

Never tiring, you carry on reading,
hunt well on beyond the dusk,
bill-boarding the silence with thickets
of headlines, until you come
to my early release, and all the other
mice they've let out on license.
An infestation - they say - due to rally
in the Free Trade Hall next Monday
week. You pass it over for me to see,
seconds later I watch as you slip away
in the undercurrents of sleep.

WHEN YOU ARE UNHAPPILY MARRIED

how do you answer someone
who whispers *Are you real?*
Then reaches out a hand -
and you, honeyed at the slight
tremors in their fingers,
humming birds saying,
for weeks now I've dared
myself to touch you.

And I had to look away
because you wouldn't stop staring
but I could feel your hands
simultaneous, moving
with your voice in tow,
soothing, saying *sit still,*
it seems an age since I did this.
And you filled your hands
with my hair
and I shut my eyes..

After you kissed me
nothing that sounded
like reason came out of my mouth,
but my Gulliver's heart snapped
from its stakes and I struggled
to sit up, right myself, my head
like a globe on a stand, reeling
as I fought to take control

of my unruly hair that flew,
like wild horses in a circus ring
around my face, un-tethered.
Imagine, after all that training
my whole married body, straining.

MAKING CALICO CANVASES FOR HEDDLE

You have no money
but still it doesn't stop you,
doing this for your daughter.
You're good with your hands,
you turn them over, raw earth,
palms up like serving hands
for a salad bowl, spreading
your fingers, flexing
the space between,
so that light passes through
like Autumn in maple.
You use what you have
to hand, to make her canvasses.

Off cuts of a pine bed,
make oblongs, squares,
slub calico does for scrim
across the frame.
You stretch it tight
until it groans, gives in,
then you staple it or tack it
round with carpet tacks,
until it sounds hollow when tapped,
like an unbroken hymen.

You watch her paint, astonished.
In her hands banks of green cypresses
are teenage girls wriggling in lycra dresses,

lighting up, like emeralds do,
the bare throats of her canvasses,
and the plain room you're both in,
glitters like an embassy dinner.

When she's satisfied she hands it to you.
How best to put it,
into words or paint, the opening lines
of an epic poem or letter;
you should have seen her smile,
your smile. Both broke, slipping very slowly,
like raw eggs into a see through bowl, mingling,
clinging like a good vintage to its glass.

THERE'S NO TALKING THROUGH THIS

Pomander

I knew that what we said
that Autumn day, as we sat upstairs
on the sofa, the view fanning
russet, tabby, tussling in the vicious wind
like a tawny owls wing-
that the right words we dished out,
passed like pomanders between us-
couldn't break curses or work black magic,
wouldn't be enough.

Salvage

My hands ingenious did
what my words couldn't.
The mermaid's purse, twin
stump work pearls,
cutting, pinking, tacking,
neatly knotting and stitching
back the bladder wrack
the night trawler.
dragged from inside you.

Seahorse

Swathes of sweat
made great strides across
your face, neck
as you bent double.

I leant over you, one hand
spanned your forehead as your
head drooped over the toilet bowl.

I gathered up your hair, frisky
as a colts pony tail it bolted,
a hundred volts, swishing
away swarms of finger nails.

I soothed, steadied
you with my voice. I watched
as you spewed, life ebbing out
of you like a sea horse giving birth.

Gift

You rallied round, requested another pillar
be put behind your head, asked for a glass of water,
you fancied something to eat, two courses, one savoury,
one sweet. You sat up, Mona Lisa smiled, we watched
daylight anew, how it jestered, tousled the duvet
as an elders hand ruffles a child's head.
We talked, laughed, wept and everything we said
sounded skylark clear, felt like a woodcut, uncluttered.
And the room's dimensions altered, became alpine
when the two of us, maidens, set to, tended to you,
flung back the shutters to an audience of meadow flowers.
Later, when night nipped in, slipped off its cloak,
cast a few stars, spangled bars across the sky,
you gave us the only gift you had left.

Perm

We'd never met until this hour,
and now such intimacy.
The shoulder of my astrakhan coat
grazing, nudging against you,
black brains they spewed onto
the thick seams of your tweed coat.

Felled, a great oak, six bearers
bore you with dignity, Liverpool pride.
Outside a crowd of plaster faces bled,
though no miracle stepped forward
or ushered tidings.

This close he was as you described-
how I'd imagined, and for a split second
I saw you rippling like a light perm
beneath his fell-side bones, stubbly skin.
Sleeting looks, I stood back, let him pass,
away to the waiting cars, immediate family.

Southern Cemetary Visitors Map

At the gate lodge I hand
over your name like rent,
to a woman who says,
it's not coming up on the screen,
I'll try again, then asks,
you couldn't spell it out for me?

Outside clutching a map
I traipse round isobars
of paths, that fill the grid,
to your plot, where you seep,
flanked on either side
by a Pole and a Ukrainian,
the three of you packed,
embedded in the face of an arrowhead.

STOMACHER

A level stare at the ordinary as he leaves the house.
The air aches with heat and the narcissi seep,
faint apertures of pheasants eye, in a cut leaded glass,
but I don't stir until I hear the car move off.
I have one hour to bathe, a glass of wine stains

my throat, décolletage going wide and deep.
Time to buff my toes, vanilla my feet. I stayed
in town all winter. In the park we walked Belfast
everyday. The pond went platinum under an ice sun,
and when the seagulls came and shadows

bottled green against the yew we turned back.
If there was a hiding place in my shoe
I'd slip you in; I know what you feel like, a bloom
of red that gives warmth to silk. Time rolls like a muff
around my wrist. In a small room a changeling sleeps.

The days were plain and untrimmed till you came.
I was a long bodice partly sewn to a skirt, a hem picking
up everything. I have half an hour left. I partially dress.
The bed is a deep breath, my hair a mound of flothers, combs.
Before he left we talked through the cut and finish.

The way it can be darned and patched. I think I said *yes*.
But moments are banners and move on. And now you are here
I am a bodice intact. You place yourself, broad as a scald,

between the break of my breast bone. Sweet as a blister I weep,
burn to your touch. My belly rumbles for trinkets and nipple kisses.

As your hands close, you caress each steel band, softening bones.
No wood block with its chastity of resist, full frontal composition,
a stork feeding her young, can deny me this. My flesh gives,
sea visions, tree visions. And when you go out and he comes in,
I never fan an eyelid, look straight ahead, detached and certain.

*Stomacher: The stiffened bib worn over bodice, worn over the front of a
corset.*

ENGLISH BOOK

Five years in a classroom
and they bear no tide mark,
up to date with the latest thinking,
monitored, police vetted,
or so they say. They are quick
to reassure me, they speak the
right words, their intent I'm
sure is noble and fine, the three
of them sit upright, perfect spines.
But from the tip of the chaired circle,
where everything peters, runs out,
one woman on the selvedge shifts,
the expression in her eyes, rolls out
a length of pity, flecked with heartfelt.

She hands me his English book,
his writing butchered by punctuation,
a noose around the neck of his spelling,
her pen an axe over his syntax,
scrawls of red through the jazz
of his sequencing, pages piled with offal.
From her, not a shred of tender meat,
or a sign that she understands, though
I tried to show them; the oracle
in his entrails, and what beats at its centre.
A starved lion-cub waiting for a word kill.

BROTHERS

At the sight of *Field*
one of you sank to your knees,
got out a Reeves sketch book,
and squatting between the open legs
of the door frame,
in awe of orange began to draw.
And the other, cool, measured,
direct, pea shot his gaze,
for a split second, no more,
before winding himself like a beanstalk
round the room, making for the window,
and a collection of tall ships moored
in the dock. I'm patiently waiting,
flicking through chained catalogues
on a window seat, while a strange man
in a hat stoops, categorically states
it's a dole queue in Belfast, late 50's.
From the corner of my eye,
I notice you both, one still drawing,
the other shuffling, growing edgy,
twenty minutes down the line, telling
someone who asked, *What do you think?*
that *it's ok, but which one's special?*

FLORENTINES

(for Tom)

I make us two strong coffees.
Like Venetian merchants
pulling the cords of their
purse strings we grab chairs,
draw ourselves
round the kitchen table,
our knees butting.

Cup to my lips my pitchfork eyes
toss a florin for you to go first.
She was young, single
worked in a framework knitters factory-
Nottingham-that these days
makes dodgy lingerie.
He was a student, a casual waiter
in Summer doing the rounds
in a Guiseppe ice cream van.
I nod, not much difference there,
except mine were older, over here-
he on restaurant business,
her a student nurse at the time.

A windfall of light relieves
the winter darkness.
You open two buttons on your shirt,
steep sloping terraces of chest hair.
I run my fingers through vintages

of my hair, both of us knowing
a knee length boot has trampled there.

We try and laugh it off,
hold our hands up, mime,
we forgive, but our child-talk
seeps to relief like the weave
of damask. In different voices.
I go first, he was a famous
actor, she an aristocrat,
a socialite. You tell me
that's right. Your voice tilts,
swerves, he was a racing driver
twice winner at Le Mans,
she was stunning, birthday
list honoured, studied
at the Sorbonne, both sets tireless
campaigners for childrens' rights.

HONEYMOON AT HELENS BAY

Our feet hovercraft along the shoreline.
Wagtails ripple, arch of piano keys,
scores ahead of us. Waves edge forwards
pull backwards like a fairground machine.
You place the palm of your hand on mine,
new penny, its weight tips us, we hit
the jackpot, the sea senses, showers us
with stones, shingle, crushed shell confetti.
Around us pods of seaweed party pops,
Maypoling. Later when the sun drops
a sequin moon stitches itself to mass black,
we shed our clothes, skinny dip, wicked gods
we flirt with the rise and fall, breathless waves.

MOTHERING

When I've set up shop and I'm stood behind the counter
they come, the absolutist pacifists, socialists, suffragettes,
the obviously unfit, their faces pinched and frozen,
caught up in an avalanche, an impasse of white feathers.

Out of the Derby gloom their expressions loom,
I wait on their words, their hand and facial gestures,
I recognise these lot all added up are the total sum of mine.
Usually they ask me the basics, whereabouts

of my terraced house, the chances of a set
of lice free clothes, bed for the night, a scalding cup
of tea. Later when the shops shut up, doors bolted,
they huddle, hushed voices around the table,

discuss which passage they're on, the risks involved
in obtaining a set of false documents.
Later when all is nunnery I think of them
long gone, a husk of hares, sabreing across
wounds of fields, hoards of contacts
racing through their blood like viruses.

THE FIRST TIME

it happened,
I couldn't stop bleeding.

You acted quick like Shelley
filled the bath
with ice to suture the flow

before flooding
the room with florescent light.

SECOND TIME

Although we are nature, plentiful
as a harvest festival, we are wary
with each other.
You see my confidence
lies in doing a thousand different
things with my eyes.
Twice I have seen you use your
small body as a landscape,
gasped, as you dappled and gambolled
across the wheat field scan,
your long and short bones
emphasizing tissue mass,
against a speckled, black leaded black.

And when I can sleep, I try not
to sleep too heavily against your cusps
and curves, without the certainty
of a sturdy pillow, pit propped beneath.
On bombed out days I mock-foetus
and you rumble, roll me in like
a sacred stone, across the mouth
of a double chambered souterrain.
Your instinct; to protect me from raiders.
Then our conversations take on the colour
of elastic released from a swollen wrist
and we start to exist to each other, all over again.

When you decide to release me,
I leave the table unsided, cooker half cleaned,
though I insist on putting out the windows eyes
by drawing the blinds,
keep my hospital bag waiting. Sodden with kicks
I ease myself away like a midnight kiss.
Inside I am like an arched dome,
and a single cherub is trumpeting, swinging
from the rafters, rising to the occasion.

SQUARE IN THE LANDING CEILING

Just as she remembered, one door
opened into a square, hotch potch
of lino tiles, dimplex heater on low,
rainforest of potted plants, singer sewing
machine that needed servicing.
Then a flight of Eiger stairs, unsuitable
for a chair lift, too steep, or so the workman
said, and straight ahead another door,
another tricky lock, double agent,
three twists, the dead lock breaks,
one shove and she's in, opens,
like a pop up book into another landing.
Bigger square, laid bare, except
for a chocolate box picture
that he liked and she always hated.
Above her head a distressed ceiling,
hole in the ice, a cut out square
that she lifts as she stands on a chair.
It flaps like an advent window,
opens onto a dark winter day;
she's Oliver and knows where Fagin
keeps his treasure trove, his getaway.
So simple, stashed inside a manky Clarks
shoe box, passport, shares, Isas,
cash bricks, variety of certificates;
all play their part; blacked up they
try to disguise themselves like mummers.
Only the sound of her jewellery tinkles

as she stashes what's left inside her coat.
For this is what she's become to him,
for he's here, hiding somewhere, listening,
for she's become the rattle of a blind man
shaking his tin, town crier for lepers.

LACE SWANS

In a glass case in County Antrim
her children sit, four lace swans.
She whispers what she should have said

that they should have sailed on fine spun silk.

Blond and black boned, thread trawl,
Minonet, Hanover lace,
the quartet moored in her memory.

They should have sailed on sheer satins.

Laces worn on different occasions,
Carrickmacross guipure, playtime, games,
Carrickmacross appliqué, opera, Sabbath wear.

They should have sailed on calico.

The world overflowing with babies,
bundles of Irish lace their cries aren't crochet
or lean white damask.

They should have sailed on crepe de chine.

She pays a girl each quarter to wash her linens,
watches her hands smooth as wax,
amongst lace silk trimmings.

They should have sailed on armozeens.

The way she tosses her hair, turns her legs,
sews new feet into stockings, measures arches
heel to toe, craft of nail to quick.

They should have sailed on alapeen.

The heat of her skin, damp wool smouldering
as she stirs the pot .
Four swans glide by on a smile.

They should have sailed on calimanco

So she watches her mend, join lace to bodice,
and under her breath, she hums words,
lace, camlet, brocade, shalloon.

Words forbidden, poplins, prunella, damasks.

The names of her children surface last.
They should have sailed into another's arms,
but for the glass, the glass, the glass...

ARIA

We take her up to the cottage.
She wants to try it before
she makes a final decision,
in the same way you tentatively
taste, sniff at something
foreign like a soft cheese.
She wants to see what its like
to be on her own, not be
surrounded by a music hall
of others, vying, clicking
fingers, clamouring
for her instant attention.
She wants to negotiate
the corkscrew stairs,
in her own time, sit in
the attic, be a Puccini
heroine, Mimi or Tosca
and fantasise,
while listening to a chorus
of rooks warming up in the Gods
of La Scala, absorbing
the dark acrid scents,
the angles, pitched wings
make as they strut and fan
against the sweeping
branches, props of Scot's pines.

INCREDIBLE

By chance we collide
on High Pavement, outside
The Galleries Of Justice.
And yes, you're still enclosing spaces.
Me, Oh you know, still dressing people.
Field walkers at the end of a deep furrow
we take a break, step into the road,
let the frantic masses pass.
We kick around the past.
Words like thick clods of Anglo Saxon clay
cling from the soles of our shoes.
Our talk forges on, mines
until eventually we strike
an old seam, discover its still rich in finds,
and the air's sweet with gases thickening,
and look, the birds are still breathing.

EXECUTION

I was sitting, waiting outside,
my knees nestling underneath
the rim, cold silver rind of the café table,
when something I don't know
made me lathe your way,
and I watched as you rippled
smoky behind the plate glass,
swash-buckling, going the distance
with the waitress,
and I could feel my smile
like wax weeping,
melting my mouth
into nothingness, like shortbread.
I didn't dash off a note in lipstick,
or leave a jolly tip for old time sake.
No, that would have been
like fox scent, a big mistake.
I walked away threading
through the silent gaping crowds,
until I turned the corner,
and the sound
that crept through my ears,
coursed through my head,
was the solid groan of the crowd
signalling, *The King Is Dead.*

CIGAR

I must want it because
this is the third time this week.
You draw me out the way that salt
releases pent up sun from a tomato.
You take me through you, step by step.
When I'm not with you,
this is how you sit, how you swivel
your hips, stretch out your legs.
You lift my hand so it hovers
like a hummingbird over your nectar face.
You close your eyes. Sloth,
you ray my fingers, take two, press
them like Venetian glass to your bottom lip.
Drenched by my hair you whisper
into my ear as if speaking through
the intricate filigree of a grill.
I only have to think of you to see you.
I've heard this one before.
Snap. A swell inside my head,
a neap tide remembers again
as you come behind me,
a lantern slide and George Sand
is smoking her thin cigars.
She blows me words,
drowns me in a hoop-la
of Havana kisses.
Your eyes, grisly animal traps,
spring open and you're leading me

like a dancing bear to your desk,
that when I fool around with the lid,
before I sit on it, leaks the clawing
aroma of smoke, and I'm thinking
hold on don't take your jacket off,
I'm not ready - yet.

BOY MORE THAN WILLING TO BE CAPTURED

On those deep ochred days when the air
complies with the sky darkening,
when the daffodils glow,
and soft rain softens, smudges
the surface of every leaf
it stumbles across,
I recollect the moment
I so consciously weighted,
contemplated, like a beach stone,
or the flounced head of a rain
sequined rose at dusk,
when one day you'd come into your own.

As I drove along the narrowing lane,
thinking I'd surprise you,
pick you up from the party,
the seed heads rattled in that second
when our seasons changed,
and not a passion or a phase,
or a pumpkin split, quartered.

I highlighted you with my headlights,
beyond the yellowing grass,
an Oxford stripe running like
a river down the lanes centre parting,
below the overhanging branches
of sloes, slow drumming the roof
of the car; me showing didn't throw you.

You had come this far,
this last leg, on your own.
The only boy they'd invited
to the party, caught up in a web
of handkerchief sleeves, a scene
from a Richard Dadd, you waved
to me, cool, intoxicated, fronting
the backdrop they'd created,
booze, fumy perfumes of oriental grasses.

You, wondering at the way they looked,
the way their talk touch-stoned
one another, nuzzled into their secret
hiding places like sphagnum moss.
Backing away, out of sight,
I saw the conscious handing
over of the baton, a hand
transferring a willow pattern.
Folding my voice away like a napkin
I placed you inside my chest
like a flower pressed.

.

FERRAGAMO'S INVISIBLE SANDAL

You said *take off your kitten heel mules.*
So I did, thinking why not? Here we go.
And you took up my foot, tried to slipper
it into the palm of your hand. My foot
was too big, my toes overhung like a fringe.
With your free fingers you swabbed, whispered
this is where the latchets, vamps should go.

I thought latchets, vamps, now you're talking.
In between you reminisced about fishing
on Strangford Loch. I sat pretty, concentrating
on your words, as you probed my instep.
Breast, sole, top-piece, the arch of my foot dolphining,
I only bit when you told me how another man,
an Italian who also loved fishing, made
the most incredible shoes inspired

by watching fishermen casting across the Arno.
How during the Second World War,
leather was made over to soldiers boots,
so shoemakers made sandal uppers from hemp,
straw, raffia, sea grass, making feet look feral.
You said you read about him in prison.
The Maze. You never raised your eyebrows or blinked,
just kept tracing your fingers across the top

of my foot, criss-crossing the espadrille laces
of my veins. I branded my eyes into your skull.
I'm not afraid to talk about my stint between
the war years. See, Ferragamo, he relished working
with restrictions. I see parallels, like being banged
up in a cell, free to pioneer unusual materials.
For him it was cellulose.
For me? Now that would be telling.

ORANGERY AT CROM

The Lough is aware of us, our vibrations.
It intercepts the tenancy of our footsteps,
our boot-sole imprints, by closely lapping,
overlapping the shoreline, navigating
its water rhythms, an abundance of demi-waves,
through mounds of spear headed reeds.
We are travellers aware we have
passed this way before. We walk on
to Old Crom Castle. Across the Erne Gads Island,
a sliver of ice embedded in a pure wool mist.
Out toward the island of Inisherk a pair of coots,
sirens of shrieks, fracture and crackle the mist
where water fowl shapes distress the surface
like the surface of a poorly conserved old master.

The River intensifies its waves like a perm,
ushers us into its focal point, a near perfect
view for this waterside Orangery.
Inside its honeycomb room, through fine gentrified
glazed window bars, we look out from one side
onto a river amassing, and from another to mosses,
densely planted with the melancholy up lights
of yellow aconites, a torch light of white narcissi.
You say we could squat here for a while
and before I answer you are gathering rare
lichen covered logs, foraging for kindling sticks
to light the fire, a hearth bonfire big enough
to roast a poached Doe on.

MY MOTHER, MY HUSBAND

A massive stroke of bitter cold,
the moor tops slipped, white stricken
down one side in the night.
Yet still we walk towards
the acupuncture of Nine Ladies,
ringed by silver, a psoriasis of flaking birch.
My boys run on, a tingle of nerve endings,
every limb jerking, flashing, electrocuted
by the sight, an unexpected fall of snow.

I lag behind watch as she points
to the soles of her city shoes,
sheepishly indicating no grip.
Fine chain, I think, you have a duty
to link her. She pats your arm,
her fingers linger, ramble
a little too long for my liking
into the dell, swell at the elbow
where the fold of your jacket gathers.

Getting ahead of me, I watch
the side of her face turn, sunning itself
on the spirit white of your breath,
the deep lines, thick contours,
ancient mapping out of her skin
obliterating like a premature Spring
in front of me.

HEIGHTS OF ABRAHAM

Minutes before the curtain drops,
the sky spans raspberry ripples,
fans herself for effect. Clouds muster
their slow descent over High Tor,
a mass of overhead mantillas,
they drape the lacquered roundel
not yet settled behind the crag.

We walk across the drowsy meadow,
gaze at its pock-marked face,
from the other side.
Cut loose you are first to the summit,
you plant your smile in my eyes
as if it were a flag.

Knees bent you compress
the circulating air,
tuck yourself in,
into a foxglove hollow,
lying in wait.
Seconds later I join you.
Bleats of figurine sheep

echo through the gorge,
orchids stipple, rooks tighten
their crampon legs to ledges
as the scenery shifts.

Flat backs we squat,
attend to the sunset with all our senses.
A hawthorn twists a barb in the corner

of your eye as the sun dunks
by degrees into Indian blue inks.
My fingers run through your wild flower hair,
you're never too big for this.
You reach out -
not for your school books, globes,

cosmic spheres, charts,
scientific maps, animal A B C-
you reach out to revolve your fingers
through slakes of sun rays,
feeling for a winter berry,
thinking yourself inside
the throat of a rosehip.

SHIRT BANDS

I knew exactly what they were
when I bought them for you.
On the day of your birthday
I served you breakfast in bed,
gave you presents.
I watched you rifle through
the wrapping paper, stop,
before fingering them one by one.
Goading you I said, *Guess?* as you
unthreaded the fine twine that linked them.
Your voice, like a thin line, broke.
Hair bands for a bloke,
is this some sort of joke?
I inched closer, slipped
them over your wrists.
Perfect fit. Jacquard weave,
a snake skin shed, threaded
through with springs. Ease.
A tight rope crossed this time.
Wait. The wardrobe gapes.
Come here, close the door,
show me again how you do it?

SON, WON'T YOU AT LEAST

allow me this one small act of tenderness-
let me sew that button onto your shirt.
It's not a sign of weakness
to have me lean over your shoulders-
say, *give it here*-
And I hold my arms out like a barrier crossing,
trying to breach the divide that's materialised,
like a heavy goods train between us.
Reluctantly you hand it over
like it's a good days takings from the till,
give me that look, that goes with all the others
you've totted up, the one that says
you want receipts. All things taken
into account I hold back what's
inside my head. If I said, *take it or leave it,*
I'd be seen as the one giving the lip.
So I take a step back, toss my head,
bowl a whopping smile, that says *whatever,*
more spin on it than a cricket ball.
Hands on my hips I wait for you to knock
it back like banter, or six. Instead you shove
past me, and I reel back, watch
as you near take the door off its hinges,
go your own way out the back,
kicking over the fields with your feet-
the odd remnants left between us.

THE MATCH BREAKER

She handled me with skill,
setting me down on a chair,

as if I were a dare at a country fair,
to poke fun at.

See, she had to be careful, had to
think of her son; men from The West

were in her family. See, it could be
nestling in my genes, lurking cobalt,

riddling a changeling seam,
like the Sicilian fairy, Caroline Crachami.

What if it bounced back or skipped
a generation, lay dormant, predatory

in a chrysalis memory? Not easy to untie,
the old wives tale from modern medicine.

She mithered, what could be done if things
backfired in this God forsaken country?

She brewed some tea, waited
patiently for me to settle.

See, your Mother was a fervent believer
that maternal impressions caused freaks.

Telling me the story about an artilleryman
with a hare lip, club feet,

who robbed a pregnant woman
on the open road- bold.

A months cycle to the day,
and a baby born with a face

of brown down, the silky sneer of a leveret.
Then there was the monkey that made itself

at home, between a young girls
thighs, that bit her fingers

when she touched herself, surprised,
threw her into fits, so she nearly died.

But the truth is she was terrified,
I could see it, Rumplestiltskin in her eyes.

She couldn't face it, let him risk giving her
a Grandchild, weighing one pound,
measuring seven inches.

* Caroline Crachami, also know as the Sicilian Fairy, was once Britain's most
famous Dwarf. Her skeleton is on show in the Hunterian Museum in London, part
of the Royal College of Surgeons, where she stands next to the Irish Giant,
Charles Byrne

PRACTISING ON YOUR MOTHER

He is still at the age
where he kisses me willingly.
Some days he alights on my lips,
takes me by surprise
like an Emperor butterfly,
his fine china lips,
hot tipsy with heat.
Hard, slightly apart,
he presses his lips to mine
and I feel them print
like a butter mould.
Tenderly I push him away.
He leaves me pink champagne
bubbles in slicks of silvery saliva
as he rushes out to play.
I force myself to wipe it away,
But before I do I can't resist
lotusing, folding my lips
in on my tongue,
like a geisha tasting,
and I taste a taste
that's familiar, that sweetens,
that's complicated for me.
He's not far away, I hear him
kicking his football beneath
the window, I shoo him away.
He looks at me half heartedly,
as though he sort of understands.

KISSING THE SHUTTLE

We tough it out in rough grass,
heavy blanket stitch our way
over lichen pox kerb stones
with muddy boots, a last ditch attempt
to stem what's left from further fraying.

What use is a millrace without
the working flax mill, you say.
I brand my hand in your coat pocket.
Tough as a mule you're true to your word,
set to, prepare its neglected foundations,

wade through a single malt river, carrying
each stone, high above your head
like loaded muskets. And because of your peoples
presence, their grains, gradients inside the rock,
they begin to heat, spit-sizzle like the ancient

songs, and by the time you clamber
up its banks, light a fire, post sentries
at either end, erect ditches, balustrades,
kiss each stone you lift like a shuttle
to life, the stones rise to something

like blood heat, so you pass them along the line,
not in an attempt to dampen a blazing fire, no,
more like the way the hands of a community,
pass baskets of fresh baked bread to break the siege,
nourish the culture of a starving people.

ZEAL

I saw you come out of the bank
and it was as if I had stepped
into the seventeenth century
and someone's breasts seared
against the side of my face,
their hands busy, plumping
pillows beneath my head.
And I could feel colour soak
away from my face, making
my eyesight sharp as the scalpel
that bled me, led me
to believe that my senses
were divine, mystic, drawn
from a sacred well, up towards
the rim of my lips, like elixir,
and it was going to be so simple,
all I had to do was wave myself
like a wand in front of you.

SOMETHING BETWEEN LARNE
& CAIRNRYAN

Sent to the back of the boat with the smokers
I listen for the umpteenth time to you
say *listen, its for the best.*
Perhaps I should tip my head to one side,
like a trilby or open my eyes
wide open like a laboratory chimp.

I remember times when I licked the knotted
words from your lips like clotted cream,
swelling on their nourishment; I couldn't stop
turning over your turn of phrase the like of which
I'd never heard before, and as for all
your skyscraper stories: Yes, I believed them.

But your attempt at saying *It's for the best,*
this attempt at second best, doesn't hang
in the air for long, they're just words
so easily pulled to pieces like mohair,
and I hang on to the handrail as the boat
aborts first the land then the loch for the sea.

You raise your hand, as if to bless me,
it's come down to this. You won't go back,
or bring yourself to reassure yourself
by kissing me. I move away. You walk the deck
as if it were the Jolly Rodger, No that's unfair,
you walk in a way that says *So this is it.*

DRESS SHIRT

I didn't have a washing line
to peg out your Rocola dress shirt,
so I improvised, shawled it around
the topiary triangle of a bay tree.
Later, when I looked at it,
held it white up to the sky,
it rustled, billowed O in the breeze
like an eighteenth century balloon's first flight.

Briskly I inspected damp suckers,
one here - and there - and there,
where the suns flat iron had missed.
Then I brought it in,
throwing it over my shoulder
like a matador, to a room
where a summer fire was lit,
and where I'd placed a maiden-
several paces back -
so as not to scorch the wood,
its legs splayed, in waiting
for smalls, trivial light things.

I stood before its breath,
my face smeared with pheromones.
Between my fingers and thumbs
I held the shirt out, it swooped
like a cartoon ghost steaming.
Full on it smelt of privet flowers,

the breeze having buttered
it relentlessly on both sides.
My thoughts thickening like sauce
I imagined you later that night,
wearing it, its moon shine up against
your black dinner jacket lining,
wondering about the smell,
cupping your breath in the urinals.

WHITE PEAK

The car still moving we scan
the grasses' seed heads,
a weight of startled exclamation marks.
You are compelled to stop
by the pin-point of a hawk,
an air-borne crucifix set against
the marble biased dusk.
The engine turned off,
we listen as the White Peak silvers,
whitens, spreads its silence.
You, in your journeyman way take
my hand and walk me away,
over uncut quarries, through drowsy
flowers where our eyes fill
with unwindings of dandelions,
cowslips, lady's smocks.

WELL DRESSERS

Shippon doors flung open in waiting.
We murmur into our hands, watch
the men haul soaked screens
from the village pond. The clay
dug fresh from Tissington wood,
shared out between five wells,
squats puddled with salt for softness,
in clefts of mossy stoneware sinks.
Windmills of hands, we work attentively,
tack nails, sweep trowels, key
the clay up to an inch thick.

Carried inside on the shoulders of Peaklanders,
we roll the vetted drawing out. Collectively
we bed down the clay face, steadily
we prick out, tooled up with awls,
a spiked dressmakers wheel, cocktail sticks,
bodkins, hat pins, we prod-prick.

Fired up by last years Autumn
we gathered black knobs in advance;
holly, snow, rowan-berries, spears
of larch twigs. Peeling away the paper,
admiring our handiwork of open pores,
we make the outlines course.
Dressers we begin filling in.
When shadowing, we use the heavy
weights, barks, mosses, reeds, electrified

lichens, and sometimes crushed fluorspar.
Botanists we colour code our flowerings.
Heads bent, fingers cat cradling,
petalling, each petal clinkered into place,
a language preened like Braille. Hypnotic.
In cycles we murmur into our hands
How hard the Puritans tried.

* *A Peaklander is a native of Derbyshire.*

BOY WITH ANGELICA STICK

Lay flat on his back his hair has the movement
of kelp in a heavy swell, his eyes smart
like Ulster's tides, under a nineteen twenties
ovum lamp. So I cover the shade with a square

of Chinese silk, relieved that his far shore kin
cannot see him scissoring his stick, from left
to right. I see the rapidity of his S's, his capacity
to whistle gaily through leaf moulded fingertips,

uplifting 50p boulders along the way; an unknowable
way that he has yet to reinvent, before venturing.
I think about his stick, how he grew it from biennial
seed, watched it burst for a native bird

into a mustard beaded planet, harvested the stem,
left it to season, drilled some holes, painted it
like a Nohkan, played it down in the cellar,
a double chambered souterrain of boys.

I remember the day he came to me clutching a fistfull
of family photographs. A big old house with a plaque,
a traditional garden that sustained an apple orchard
for secret meetings. He sees landscapes, faces outside

the boundary of his memory. But there's the spark in his eye
that reads, *words rubbed together make heat*, as his feet kick
the air into ribbons and pleats, and now he's overland heading
for the sea, his voice far ranging, ranting and raging

on how he no longer wants his stick to be called a stick,
when its name - its rightful name - is a baton, and a drum -
his drum - is no longer any old drum, but a Lambeg.

* *Nohkan is a wooden Japanese flute*

CHINA BOWL

As she suspects the bowl is fine
finer than any of the other objects in the room.
It sits on the windowsill facing
a Nicholson harbour.
She pulls up a chair, scours the sea
like a fisherman's widow.
Her eyes dragnet, sink into the water,
molten, blue, bluer, deeper.
Pulling herself away she runs her fingers
round the rim of the bowl, a cold brilliant
cusp of desolation,
knowing if she presses hard it'll snap
like crème brûlée, so she sets it down.
Opening a window she smokes,
the waves are a dark soliloquy falling.
Newlyn lights up- up lights her face,
she walks to the door, walks back,
picks it up, tests it like one of her
longer poems, taps it with her fingernail,
listens to it ring,
hold on to its song for so long.

THE WAY I DRESSED DURING
THE REVOLUTION

The day that took too long to come arrived.
The self-drive van came down the street,
arched its armoured back; it sees me,
a feverish chant flowing out
of the mouth of a town house.

I had difficulty deciding which stripe,
red, blue or white, which national trophy,
which bunch of tricoloured flowers to press-
symbolically - to my left breast. I ran my hands
down my plain skirt, straight lines that started
at the high waistline, usurped the hoop,

the bodice cut short to the waist, sleeves
to the elbow; I kept the neck low, finished off
with fichu. Silk, velvet, ribbon, lace,
driven out by cotton, an act of solemn decree;
something for us later to disagree on.

And to keep my hair from straying on the deck,
a mob cap, nick-named Charlotte Corday,
irritating deep ruffles around the face,
a scarlet cockade I astutely placed, in case
on arrival in the North we hear
of a sudden accession.

Done and dusted, my manner of living
simplified, the contents of the house
wrenched from my arms like a baby,
wrapped, strapped down in the back,
my goods and chattels lying in state.

I climb in, look back in anger,
and people are mingling,
batches of tiny brown hens;
a few still defiant, pecking for glamour.
We take to the road, make for the quay
and the all night crossing.